John Currey

The Terry-Broderick Duel

John Currey

The Terry-Broderick Duel

ISBN/EAN: 9783337138790

Printed in Europe, USA, Canada, Australia, Japan

Cover: Foto ©ninafisch / pixelio.de

More available books at **www.hansebooks.com**

THE
TERRY-BRODERICK DUEL.

WRITTEN BY

HON. JOHN CURREY.

FORMERLY CHIEF JUSTICE OF THE SUPREME COURT OF CALIFORNIA.

———————

ALSO THE

ORATION

OF

COLONEL EDWARD D. BAKER

OVER THE DEAD BODY OF DAVID C. BRODERICK,

SEPTEMBER 18, 1859.

———— ◆ ————

WASHINGTON, D. C.:
GIBSON BROS., PRINTERS AND BOOKBINDERS.
1896.

THE TERRY-BRODERICK DUEL.

It is now more than thirty years since the world-renowned duel between David S. Terry and David C. Broderick transpired, in which the latter fell mortally wounded. Before proceeding with a detailed account of this terrible tragedy and the immediate circumstances and causes which led up to it, it is proper to notice the condition of society in California in the earlier days and the political state of affairs during the first decade of the state's history.

During the year 1849, and for a few years thereafter, there was a large immigration to California from nearly all the states of the Union. They were mostly young men under forty years of age, who came seeking fortunes in this new and promising land. Many were ambitious for political distinction and regarded California as a promising field for political enterprise. Of the latter class, the southern states furnished the larger proportion, and they came fully impressed with the belief that they were the superiors of the northern men in the qualities of gentlemen born to rule, and therefore the party leaders and directors of political affairs were to be found mainly in the ranks of these southern gentlemen, some of whom before coming to California had held public positions of honor. They believed in slavery as a beneficent institution, and for the most part regarded the "Code of Honor" as an appropriate means for the settlement of personal grievances. They considered a southern man greatly superior to one of northern birth and education, in prowess and courage and in the skilful use of deadly weapons, and consequently there were many duels, first and last, in a considerable number of which a northern man was one of the combatants, who, notwithstanding his northern origin and education, manifested a courage and skill which more than astonished his hot-headed adversary. The experience of a few years taught this presuming class of southern young men that latitude and longitude were not safe criteria for the determination of courage and skill. They soon learned that whether born and reared in the highlands of the North or on the plantations of the South, "A man's a man for a' that."

It is just to say of the immigration from the south, that many were gentlemen of high educational attainments and of refined and cultured manners. In social life they were attractive and genial companions, considerate of the opinions of others. This class of gentlemen was quite unlike the pretentious and boasting middle-rank and low-grade chivalry, who were wont to carry upon their persons pistols and knives, with which, for even slight affronts, they professed themselves disposed "to blow the top of your head off."

Mr. Broderick came to California from New York early in 1849 and took up his residence in San Francisco. He was ambitious and inclined to political life. He was a stonecutter by trade, which he followed as his vocation during his early manhood. In his habits he was not prone to any of the popular vices of the day. In these respects he maintained his integrity during all his residence in California. He was a man of strong natural ability, and possessed an indomitable will and the power of drawing men to him as a leader. He was elected to the Senate of the first legislature of California, and during its second session was the presiding officer of the body of which he was a member, as the Lieutenant Governor had succeeded to the office of Governor, made vacant by the resignation of Peter H. Burnett, who had served as Governor only half of the term for which he was elected.

Dr. William M. Gwin, who came to California in 1849, was a southern man by birth, residence, and education. His sympathies were with the people of his native south, and with their "peculiar institution" of slavery. He was a man of vigorous intellectual force, and was in the early days of California the leader of his party. The first legislature of the state elected him an United States Senator, and in casting lots for terms, he drew that which expired in March, 1855. His position as a Senator added to his strength as leader of the Democratic party. His influence was exercised for the advancement of his friends to the offices of federal patronage, and, in the disposition of them, men of southern birth and education, all other things being equal, were preferred. To be eligible to office, either federal or state, it was essential, as a general rule, to be sound on the question of slavery, according to the standards of Senator Gwin and his southern allies. This was carried to such an extent during the administrations of Pierce and Buchanan, that the Custom House at San Francisco came to be known as the " Virginia Poor House."

Mr. Broderick's power as a leader steadily increased. His following comprised people from every part of the Union, though its principal strength was from the states north of " Mason and Dixon's line." As his power grew, the opposition of Senator Gwin and his southern followers and pro-slavery allies from northern states increased and strengthened until it became furious ; but Broderick was equal to the emergency, and his following grew stronger and stronger and as earnest and vehement as that of its adversaries.

In the summer of 1853, at the Democratic state convention held at Benicia for the nomination of a state ticket, the two factions of the party measured swords. The southern wing, which was called the *Chivalry*, was led by several of Senator Gwin's lieutenants, scarcely inferior in political generalship to himself. Broderick was there in person and conducted the fight against his opponents with great adroitness as well as boldness. His ticket was nominated, with John Bigler, a native of Pennsylvania, then Governor of the state, at its head. This ticket was elected, and Broderick was then regarded by the majority of the Democratic party as its leader in the state, though the Gwin or Chivalry wing yielded an unwilling acquiescence.

At the session of the legislature assembled at Benicia early in 1854, Broderick and some of his friends attempted to force on the election of a United States Senator to succeed Dr. Gwin, whose term was to expire in March, 1855. This movement was regarded by many of Broderick's friends, and others, as an injudicious and reprehensible step, as it was an attempt to do by that legislature a duty which properly appertained to the legislature to be chosen at the next election. The attempt failed.

The legislature which assembled at Sacramento, the new capital of the state, in 1855, made an ineffectual effort to elect a Senator. No one candidate could obtain a majority. The same thing occurred again at the legislature which convened in 1856. This was the " Know-Nothing " legislature, composed of Democrats, and Whigs whose organization had at that time become virtually extinct.

The Know-Nothing party grew and became dominant in the state in 1855. It was composed largely of the Chivalry branch of the Democratic party, and Whigs who had become scattered for want of a fold in which to gather them in united force.

By means of the Know-Nothing organization, the opportunity came to the Chivalry to overthrow Broderick and his close followers. David S. Terry, a resident of Stockton, was a strong pro-slavery Democrat. He had resided in Texas from his early boyhood until he came to California in 1849. He abandoned his party and became a leading Know-Nothing, and was nominated at its state convention in 1855 for Justice of the Supreme Court, to fill out the term of Alexander Wells, then deceased. He and all others on his ticket were elected, and he entered upon his office on the first of January, 1856.

The Know-Nothing party was short-lived, for in the fall of 1856 the Democratic party, then under the leadership of Broderick, gained the ascendency, and elected a legislature strongly Democratic. At its session in January, 1857, Broderick was elected United States Senator for the term to commence on the 4th of March of that year. There was also the partly unexpired term, which commenced on the 4th of March, 1855, to be filled, and Dr. Gwin and Milton S. Latham were aspirants for the position. The struggle between them for it waxed strong and bitter. Each sought the aid and influence of Broderick, who at the time had them at his feet. Broderick preferred Dr. Gwin, and he was elected. He humbly acknowledged his indebtedness to Broderick for his timely and effectual assistance. This was done in a communication over his own name, addressed to the people of California, after he was elected.

While this Senatorial struggle was in progress, there was going on in the territory of Kansas one even more vital to the cause of Civil Liberty. It was a contest between the free-state men of that territory and the pro-slavery people of Missouri and other southern states, who had gone there, some of them with their slaves, believing that this species of property, according to the doctrine of the Dred Scott decision, stood protected by the national constitution, and was as secure in their possession as any other kind of property, so long as Kansas might remain a territorial government, and always, unless the people, in their sovereign capacity, should, in the adoption of a state constitution, declare slavery to be unlawful within its borders.

The people of California had not then become generally interested in the free-state and pro-slavery contest of Kansas. In the latter part of the year, a convention of pro-slavery delegates met at the town of Lecompton, in Kansas, for the purpose of framing a constitution for the prospective state, a work which the convention performed, taking care to provide for the establishment of slavery as a permanent institution of the state. This provision of the proposed constitution was alone submitted to the electors of the territory for their adoption or rejection; but by another provision of the same instrument, the owners of slaves then in the territory were confirmed in their right in and to them, in the state of Kansas, even though the provision submitted might be rejected. The free-state men demanded a submission of the entire instrument, to be passed on by the electors of the territory, which being denied, they refused to participate in the election. The result was that the question submitted was adopted by a large majority of a very small vote cast.

President Buchanan had promised the people that any constitution which might be formed for Kansas as a state should be submitted to them for their adoption or rejection; but upon the reception of the Lecompton constitution he repudiated his pledge made to the people, and on the 2d of February, 1858, transmitted the instrument to Congress, accompanied by a special message urging the speedy admission of Kansas as a state of the Union under the Lecompton constitution, although, as he in effect expressed it, the instrument had not been fully submitted to the people for their adoption or rejection. Against admission under the proposed constitution, there arose in both houses of Congress a strong opposition, led by Senator Douglas, of Illinois, with whom was Senator Broderick, who was an uncompromising opponent of the measure. Senator Gwin exerted all his strength in support of it, and from that time the California Senators became bitter enemies. The immediate result was that Broderick fell under the ban of the administration, while Dr. Gwin came into increased favor with the President, whose sympathies were more than cordial with those in Congress who were laboring to make Kansas a slave state. Thenceforth the federal patronage for California was administered by Senator Gwin.

While the question of the admission of Kansas under the

Lecompton constitution was convulsing Congress, the whole country became intensely agitated on the subject, and the people of California soon arrayed themselves on the one side or the other of the disturbing question. Those who were strongly pro-slavery were first in the arena of the conflict; those opposed to the extension of slavery were not much behind, and the indifferent waited to see the turn of events before choosing sides. The Republicans, then a party of nascent growth in California, were to a man opposed to the Lecompton fraud, and the friends of Senator Broderick were for the most part equally so, but fully three-fifths of the people of the state were either in favor of the extension of slavery, or indifferent respecting the question.

In the summer of 1858 the Democratic party met at Sacramento and divided forces on the question of the admission of Kansas as a state under the Lecompton constitution, and questions cognate to the subject. The party from that time became two-winged, and each held its convention and nominated candidates for Justice of the Supreme Court and State Controller, the only two offices to be filled by the election of that year.

The administration wing was denominated the "Lecompton" party, and the opposition wing was called the "anti-Lecompton" party; some called it the "Douglas" party. With the anti-Lecompton wing of the Democracy, the Republicans united on the candidate for Justice of the Supreme Court; but, notwithstanding this, the Lecompton wing carried the election by a fair though not large majority.

The California Senators were in their places during the winter of 1858–'9, and each devoted his influence on the side of the question he espoused.

The leaders of the Lecompton party in California were unscrupulous as to the means which might be employed to make Kansas a slave state. They were for slavery, and hated those who boldly confronted them. They hated Broderick, for his part in the struggle, with malignant personal hatred, and no one of these pro-slavery leaders was more bitterly hostile to Broderick than was Terry, who had declared himself not only the friend of slavery extension, but also of reopening the African slave trade.

In June, 1859, the two wings of the Democracy met in state conventions at Sacramento to place in nomination each a full ticket for state officers. The anti-Lecompton wing was the first to make its nominations. At that time the California Senators had returned home, and were preparing to enter upon the approaching campaign. Judge Terry was placed before the Lecompton convention for the office of Justice of the Supreme Court, as his own successor, but he failed to receive the nomination. It fell to the lot of one of his competitors. The nominations having been completed, there was held in the hall or place of the convention, on the evening of the 24th of June, a meeting to ratify the nominations made. At that meeting Terry was called upon to speak, and he responded in a vehement speech, in which he inveighed coarsely and insultingly against the anti-Lecompton party, of which Broderick was a member and the leader in the state, and against Broderick personally. The particularly offensive part of his speech is here given He said:

"Who have we opposed to us? A party based on no principles except the abusing of one section of the country and the aggrandizement of another; a party which has no existence in fifteen states of the confederacy; a party whose principles never can prevail among freemen who love justice and are willing to do justice. What other? A miserable remnant of a faction, sailing under false colors, trying to obtain votes under false pretences. They have no distinction they are entitled to. They are the followers of one man, the personal chattels of a single individual, whom they are ashamed of. They belong heart and soul, body and breeches, to David C. Broderick. They are yet ashamed to acknowledge their master, and are calling themselves, forsooth, Douglas Democrats, when it is known—well known to them as to us—that the gallant Senator from Illinois, whose voice has always been heard in the advocacy of Democratic principles, has no affiliation with them, no feeling in common with them.

"Perhaps, Mr President and gentlemen, I am mistaken in denying their right to claim Douglas as their leader ; perhaps they do sail under the flag of a Douglas ; but it is the banner of the black Douglas, whose name is Frederick, not Stephen."

These were the words of the Chief Justice of the Supreme Court of the state, the dignity of whose position, his friends have claimed, weighed heavily upon him.

The speech was reported in the "Sacramento Union," a newspaper of wide circulation, on the morning of the following day, from which it appeared that it was received by the large audience with great applause and vociferous cheering.

This speech was the first immediate, overt offence which led to the Terry-Broderick duel,—a fact which cannot be gainsaid by any one capable of drawing just conclusions from given causes, though Terry's friends and admirers have carefully avoided giving any importance to it as an offence, one of whom has gone so far as to justify and excuse it, as clearly within the pale of legitimate debate, and in no sense censurable as a reflection against Broderick.

On the morning of the 26th of June, Broderick, while at the breakfast table of the International Hotel, in San Francisco, read the speech of Terry as it appeared in the "Union" of the 25th. He was disturbed and angered, and spoke of it to a friend next him at the table, about which there were seated a few other persons. He remarked that while Terry was incarcerated by the Vigilance Committee, he had paid two hundred dollars a week to support a newspaper to defend him, and, continuing, said : "I have said I considered him the only honest man on the Supreme Bench, but I now take it all back."

Mr. D. W. Perley, a former law partner of Terry, happened to be at the table, and resented the words of Broderick, who cut him short with some curt remark which Perley deemed offensive to himself. Perley then published his version of what Broderick said, which he endeavored afterwards to have some of those present corroborate, but met with a denial by them of the truth of his story. Perley himself challenged Broderick to a duel, which the latter declined, saying, at the time, that he would not allow himself to be drawn into an affair of the kind while the campaign then inaugurated should continue, in which it was his purpose to take a part.

Both Mr. Broderick and Dr. Gwin took the stump, and the war of crimination and recrimination between them was bitter in the extreme, and it was so to a considerable degree between the leaders of the two wings of the Democratic party, though there were exceptions to this mode of political warfare.

The election was on the 7th of September, at which the Lecompton party won a decisive victory. Throughout the campaign the air was full of imprecations and threats against Broderick. It was believed by his enemies that his death was a political necessity, and that it must be accomplished, if not by the first duel, then by another or others to follow. It is believed that Broderick himself was conscious of the dangers that awaited him, and well understood the reasons for the malignity of his enemies, for, while languishing on his dying bed, he is reported to have said : "They have killed me because I was opposed to the extension of slavery, and a corrupt administration."

Col. Edward D. Baker was with Mr. Broderick much of the time during his extreme suffering, and probably heard these words as they were uttered ; for, in his great and grand funeral oration over the dead body of his fallen friend, he repeated the dying words of Mr. Broderick, and as he continued he said: "Let no man suppose that the death of the eminent citizen of whom I speak was caused by any other reason than that to which his own words assigned it. It had been long foreshadowed. It was predicted by his friends. It was threatened by his enemies. It was the consequence of intense hatred. It was a political necessity, poorly veiled beneath the guise of a private quarrel."

While hope was entertained that Mr. Broderick might recover, a correspondent of the "Alta California" newspaper, under date of September 15th, after saying he had always been his bitter enemy, continuing, said: "I have feelings in common with mankind, and I disapprove of this man's being hunted like a dog. If he survives, other duels stare him in the face." And then he appealed to the good people of the community to join him in a protest "positively forbidding him to accept any further challenges, which will surely come should he be raised from his bed of death." These utterances of the funeral orator and the "Alta's" correspondent were but the general expressions of the people throughout the land, who believed Mr. Broderick had fallen the victim of cruel malice—a sacrifice to the political necessities of the time.

While the campaign was in its furious progress, some of Broderick's most pronounced adversaries said he must be killed, and others, more prudent in speech, ventured the prediction that he would not long survive the day of the election, and to this end they looked to Terry as the person best suited to do effective work. He, they supposed, had a pretext, if not a sufficient cause, to call upon Broderick for reparation on account of what he had said at the breakfast table.

This was the condition of things until the election was over, whereupon Terry, accompanied by his friends Dr. Ash and Dr. Aylette, on the 8th of September, the day after the election, proceeded by stage from Stockton to Oakland, having with him the pistols which were afterwards used in the duel. There they were placed in charge of a Texas friend of Terry, and thence they were taken to the field of the conflict which followed.

On the day of his arrival at Oakland, Terry addressed to Broderick, from that place, a letter, in which he said:

"Some two months ago, at the public table of the International Hotel in San Francisco, you saw fit to indulge in certain remarks concerning me, which were offensive in their nature * * *. I now take the earliest opportunity to require of you a retraction of those remarks."

To this letter Broderick promptly made answer, saying: "Your note of September 8th reached me through the hands of Calhoun Benham, Esq. The remarks made by me in the conversation referred to may be the subject of future misrepresentation, and, for obvious reasons, I have to desire you to state what the remarks were that you designate in your note as offensive, and of which you require of me a retraction."

On the 9th of September Terry answered Broderick's letter, and, complying with his request, he said: "In reply to your note of this date, I have to say that the offensive remarks which I alluded to in my communication of yesterday are as follows: 'I have heretofore considered and spoken of him (myself) as the only honest man on the Supreme Court Bench, but I now take it all back.' Thus by implication reflecting on my personal and official integrity. This is the substance of your remarks as reported to me. The precise terms, however, in which the implication was made is not important to the question. You yourself can best remember the terms in which you spoke of me on the occasion referred to. What I require is the retraction of any words which were used, calculated to reflect on my character as an officer or a gentleman."

On the evening of the same day, Broderick replied to

Terry's second letter, acknowledging its receipt, and then said: "The remarks used by me were occasioned by certain offensive allusions of yours concerning me, made in the convention at Sacramento, and reported in the 'Union' of June 25th. Upon the topic alluded to in your note of this date, my language, so far as my memory serves me, was as follows: 'During Judge Terry's incarceration by the Vigilance Committee, I paid two hundred dollars a week to support a newspaper in his (your) defence. I have also stated heretofore that I consider him (Judge Terry) the only honest man on the Supreme Court Bench, but I now take it all back.' You are the best judge as to whether this language affords good ground for offence."

To this second letter of Broderick, Terry, on September 10th, answered as follows:

"Some months ago you used language concerning me, offensive in its nature. I waited the lapse of a period of time, fixed by yourself, before I asked reparation therefor at your hands. You replied, asking for a specification of the language used which I regarded as offensive. In another letter I gave the required specification and reiterated my demand for retraction. To this last letter you reply acknowledging the use of the offensive language imputed to you, and not making the retraction required. This course on your part leaves me no alternative but to demand the satisfaction usual among gentlemen, which I accordingly do. Mr. Benham will make the necessary arrangements."

In reply to this letter tendering a challenge, Broderick acknowledged its receipt, and then said: "In response to the same, I will refer you to my friend Hon. J. C. McKibben, who will make the necessary arrangements demanded in your letter."

Here ended the epistolary correspondence, the substance of which is herein set forth, as found at length in the volume of Maj. Ben. C. Truman, entitled "The Field of Honor," and in the work of Mr. James O'Meara, entitled "Broderick and Gwin."

It is here to be noticed that the parties agreed as to the language used by Broderick respecting Terry, which he regarded as offensive in its nature. It is also to be noticed that the latter did not credit the story of his friend Perley, as to what Broderick had said at the breakfast table. Yet Mr. O'Meara, after all this, adopts Perley's version of what was said there, and deduces therefrom his conclusions that Broderick's remarks were extremely harsh and offensive.

Terry's friends have always carefully ignored the fact, that his speech before the convention of his party was to be considered as forming any part of the controversy. They assume that the remarks made by Broderick were the first offence, and have given to them an interpretation which is strained to mean that Broderick's words were an imputation against the judicial integrity of Judge Terry, which could be atoned for only by abject and craven humiliation, or by blood.

Mr. O'Meara says, in the 25th chapter of his book, that "the provocation which he (Broderick) had from Terry's remarks in the Lecompton convention was not of a character to justify a personal replication. Terry's language was directed mainly against the party of which Broderick was the acknowledged leader, and incidentally his relation to that party was mentioned, but it was simply and exclusively political; public mention and characterization, clearly within the limits of ordinary and fair debate or allusion, and without the ingredient or tinge of personality. At worst it in no wise reflected upon the character or upon the political standing of Mr. Broderick, in point of integrity or honor. But Mr. Broderick's language concerning Judge Terry was very harsh—very offensive in a personal sense; and in respect to the exalted position he occupied as Chief Justice of the Supreme Court of the state, it was intolerable to one who, in such position, was inspired with a just sense of the great dignity of the station itself, and a proper appreciation of the high duty which he owed to his associates on the bench, and the spirit which was due in upholding and vindicating the unsullied majesty of the law in its loftiest temple of the state."

This grandiloquent exaltation of the Chief Justice, who, disturbed in his dignified repose, went forth, in kindled wrath, to vindicate the unsullied majesty of the law in its loftiest temple, bates the breath. Were it not that this admiring disciple of the angered Chief Justice is known to be as deeply devoted to his hero as was Crito to his revered Socrates, it might be well suspected that his laudations were but the ebullitions of caustic sarcasm and grim irony.

This specimen passage from the work of Mr. O'Meara is but a sample of the labored efforts, from the beginning, to place Terry in the attitude of the righteous defender of personal and judicial honor, against the assault of one who had the temerity to assail, yet not the manliness to make reparation for his wrong. These efforts have consisted in the *expressio falsi* persisted in, and the *supressio veri* carefully observed, so that the impression has gained ground, to some extent, that Broderick was the first offender, and, as such, was in honor bound to make reparation; failing to do which when called upon, justly exposed him to the challenge tendered him, and justly doomed him a sacrifice upon his own altar.

To understand the merits of the controversy between the parties, the order of events should be carefully observed, from which it appears that Terry was the first to give offence. In his speech quoted, he charged Broderick and his party as being dishonest, "sailing under false colors and trying to obtain votes under false pretences;" and, in ribald and scornful terms, he denominated the anti-Lecompton wing of the Democratic party as the "personal chattels of a single

individual, whom they were ashamed of," as belonging
" heart and soul, body and breeches, **to** David C. Broderick,"
and " yet ashamed to acknowledge their master."

These were the words, not of a blackguard in private life,
but of the Chief Justice of the Supreme Court of the state.
They not only applied to the individuals of the party of
which Broderick was the leader, but to him personally, in a
most offensive sense, as a master of whom his followers
were ashamed, and as one whom they contemned **and de-
spised.**

In the correspondence between **the** parties, it appears that
Broderick referred Terry **to** the latter's speech as the *cause* or
occasion of **his** own remarks respecting him, and referred
him to the record of that speech in the " Sacramento Union "
of June 25th, the consideration of which **Judge** Terry chose
to disregard. Thus it appears that the evidence touching
this branch of the controversy between the friends of Terry
and the friends of Broderick is of the nature of record
evidence, importing absolute verity. Upon this evidence the
questions arise :

First: Which of the parties was the first to give offence ?

Second : Which **of the** parties was in honor bound **to**
apologize and make reparation to the other ?

These questions being answered, the ultimate proposition
is, Was there any just ground or excuse for the challenge
given by Terry to Broderick, even according to the principles of the Code of Honor, which the advocates of that
system for the settlement of personal quarrels maintain
are in accord with the principles of honor, justice, and
equity ?

The particularly dramatic, as well as the terribly tragic,
part of the affair, miscalled an " affair of honor," remains to
be told.

At the time the correspondence between the parties was
opened, the physical condition of Broderick was most un-
favorable for the barbarous business upon which he was called

to enter, and which he accepted. This was owing to the extraordinary mental and physical strain to which he had been subjected in the Senate, and during the political campaign then recently closed. On the other hand, Terry seemed well prepared by assiduous training for the work which he had had in anticipation for more than two months.

Both were men of great physical strength, and both of strong mental force ; but neither of them was of high educational attainments, nor of much culture. Broderick was known as a man of positive traits and giant will. He was a natural leader of men. Terry was known as a man of strong prejudices and bitter animosities. He believed in enforcing obedience to his will by force of arms. He was a natural and typical leader of the particular class to which he belonged. He believed in the Code as an appropriate means for the settlement of private quarrels. Broderick recognized its obligations, in deference to the prevailing sentiment of the time.

In Terry's first letter to Broderick he said at its close : "This note will be handed you by my friend Calhoun Benham, Esq., who is acquainted with its contents and will receive your reply." Benham delivered the letter on the evening of the day of its date, when Broderick remarked that he would give it attention the next day. Benham urged more prompt action, and from that time the correspondence proceeded at double-quick speed until its conclusion. On the part of Terry and Benham, the object seemed to be to keep Broderick under whip and spur until the work in hand should be fully accomplished. Terry's letter, tendering a challenge, was delivered by Benham to Broderick about one o'clock in the morning of the 10th of September. To effect the service of the challenge at this dead hour of the night, Benham waited on Broderick's friends at the Union Hotel, on Kearney Street, opposite Portsmouth Square, in San Francisco. Broderick was then at the house of his friend Leonidas Haskell, at Black Point, a full mile and a half away, where he had gone to obtain a comfortable rest for the night. Benham, by persistent urging, induced Broderick's polite and accommodating friends to have him aroused from his sleep, for the purpose of coming to the city on business of urgent importance. Broderick was accordingly informed of the necessity of his immediate appearance at the place appointed, and came over the hills to the city. On his way down Jackson Street, near Stockton Street, he was met by Benham, who delivered to him Terry's challenge. Broderick soon reached the hotel and there found his friends waiting his coming. He was vexed and annoyed in that they had allowed him to be disturbed and broken of his rest, of which he was sadly in need. By his letter accepting the challenge, Broderick stated the hour when it was received by him to be one o'clock in the morning.

The challenge having been given and accepted, a time and place were appointed for the hostile meeting. The 12th of September was the day named. The place designated was in San Mateo County, near the boundary line between that county and San Francisco, not far from Laguna de Merced. The principals, with their seconds, surgeons, and friends, were on the ground at an early hour in the morning. The Chief of Police of San Francisco, armed with a warrant, duly endorsed by a Magistrate of San Mateo, appeared in due time and placed the principals under arrest. They appeared before the Police Court on the same day, and, being discharged, arranged for a meeting on the following day. They met early in the morning on the 13th of the same month, at a spot near the place of their meeting the day before. The respective principals' were accompanied by their seconds, surgeons, and friends, and others curious to witness the conflict, amounting in all to about seventy.

Terry's seconds were Calhoun Benham, Thomas Hayes, and Samuel H. Brooks. Broderick's seconds were Joseph C. McKibben, David D. Colton, and Leonidas Haskell. Terry and his seconds brought with them the "Jo Beard pistols," which at that time were called the "Aylette pistols." At the same time, there appeared on the ground a gunsmith of San Francisco, with a pair of duelling pistols, his own property.

The gunsmith had been employed, by the mutual agreement of the parties, as armorer for the occasion. Mr. O'Meara and also Mr. Samuel H. Brooks, in his account of the duel, recently published in a San Francisco newspaper, speak of "Natchez," whose real name was Andrew J. Taylor, as the armorer who was on the ground of the hostile meeting. In this they are both in error. The armorer's name was Bernard Legardo. At that time Natchez had been dead nearly a year.

It is not true, as Mr. O'Meara says, that Broderick's seconds brought with them a pair of duelling pistols. They had agreed with Terry's seconds upon the armorer, and they relied upon him for suitable duelling pistols.

In the preliminary arrangements of the parties, they cast lots for the choice of pistols. The choice fell to the side of Terry, who chose the "Aylette pistols," and his seconds selected the one of the pair which they desired for his use, and handed the other to the seconds of Broderick. The armorer, Legardo, examined them and pronounced them in good order, except that they were too light and delicate on the triggers, of which fact he informed all the seconds, and told one of the seconds of Terry that the one for Broderick was lighter than the other. The armorer so testified at the Coroner's inquest upon the dead body of Mr. Broderick, and he further testified that the pistol for Broderick's use was so delicate that it would explode by a sudden jar or jerk. The armorer asked McKibben why he did not force on his principal his (the armorer's) pistols, to which McKibben replied that Terry had won the choice of weapons. The armorer then loaded the pistol to be used by Broderick, and Mr. Brooks loaded the one selected for Terry, which was delivered to him, and the one for Broderick was delivered to him, who, upon receiving it, anxiously examined it, turning it about, scrutinizing it and measuring its stock with his hand.

In Mr. Oscar T. Shuck's sketch of David S. Terry, in the "Bench and Bar in California," he gives the statement of an eye-witness to the bloody affair, written only a short time thereafter. This eye-witness said: "**Mr.** Broderick seemed to know the importance of the issue, and seemed **nerved** to meet it. **Up to the** time the pistol was handed **him, he** appeared the **cooler** and more collected of the two. **But** after examining the pistol he seemed to become uneasy. **He** betrayed nothing like lack **of** courage, but in measuring the stock of the pistol with **the** conformation of his hand, he presented **to** the observer an unsatisfied appearance. This was shown by more than one movement." **And the same** witness said: "All agreed that his personal bravery was patent. There was no weakening, but there was an anxious solicitude in his deportment that placed him at a great disadvantage." Even after the words, "Gentlemen, are you ready?" were pronounced, and Terry had responded, "Ready," Broderick spent several seconds in examining the stock of his pistol, which did not seem to fit his hand, and then he answered, "Ready," with a nod to his second, General Colton, who had announced in the beginning, "Gentlemen, are you ready?" and then followed the words, "Fire—one—two," in the measured strokes **of** the cathedral clock. Broderick fired first, as the word "one" was pronounced. Terry's shot followed at the point of time the word "two" was commenced utterance. Broderick's shot was spent in the ground some four or **five** yards in advance of him, **in** a direct line between him and his adversary. Terry's shot took effect **in** Broderick's right breast, producing a **mortal** wound, **from** which he died three days afterwards.

Upon receiving the pistol selected **for** him and loaded for use by **his** friend Brooks, Terry seemed composed, resting **it** upon his left hand **as** he held it with the other. He exhibited no concern as to its stock, formation, or shooting qualities. Until it was definitively settled that he had secured for his use the pistol of stronger trigger, the same witness said, " he seemed agitated, and measured the ground in his direction with an uneasy and anxious tread." But with his chosen pistol in hand, and the extremely delicate and dangerous one in the hands of his opponent, he took his position with firmness and composure, watching every movement and expression of his adversary.

In Mr. Brooks's account of the duel, he speaks of the appearance of the antagonists, after they had taken their respective positions, as follows : " At that time Terry appeared very cool, but Broderick showed signs of nervousness. When Colton said, ' Are you ready ? ' Terry replied promptly and clearly, ' Ready.' Broderick delayed a few moments, while he raised and lowered his pistol arm, seemingly as if it was cramped. Then he answered, ' Ready.' " This statement corroborates the accounts of others as to the character of the weapons, and Broderick's inability to suit his hand to the pistol which he was to use.

From the beginning of the correspondence until Broderick fell mortally wounded, the conduct of the Terry party was distinguished by an intensely earnest and fiercely aggressive spirit, which showed them bent on winning the fight, at all hazards. The deportment of Terry's seconds on the ground was determined, bold, and confident, which was in marked contrast with the respectful and deferential deportment of Broderick's friends, in the presence of their adversaries.

When the respective principals had taken their positions, as yet unarmed, they were each subjected to the customary examination of their persons for concealed armor. McKibben's office was to examine Terry, and that of Benham was to examine Broderick. Each of these seconds proceeded to the examination. McKibben approached Terry in a gentle and respectful manner, pressed the back of his hand against the latter's breast, and then fell back with a courtly bow and a wave of his hand. At the same time, Benham was manipulating and searching Broderick up and down his person, as if he verily believed he had upon him an impenetrable coat of mail. Broderick was greatly disturbed by Benham's conduct, and indignantly said to a friend near him that Benham had treated him as an officer with a search warrant would search a thief for stolen property. The contrast between the conduct of McKibben and that of Benham was so marked as to attract the notice of those present. Broderick's friends felt indignant as they saw him thus openly insulted, and those of them still living well remember it to this day. The examination of Broderick's person being finished, Benham stepped to the position of his principal and, covering the side of his mouth with his hand, whispered in Terry's ear, which the latter seemingly acknowledged with an approving smile.

Some time after all this, Benham acknowledged to a friend of Broderick, who took exception to his conduct and mode of examination, that it was not courteous, but excused himself on the ground that his principal's life was in his keeping, and he was bound to do whatever was necessary to protect him.

It cannot be reasonably claimed that there could be any advantage on the side of Terry in that he had the choice of pistols, *provided* they were ordinary duelling pistols and in all respects alike, and equally unknown to both parties.

It is said by those who have seen these Aylette pistols, that in stock or breech construction they are unlike ordinary duelling pistols, and the manner in which Broderick scrutinized and handled the one given him, and his efforts to fit his hand to it, was evidence that he was wholly unacquainted with it. On the other hand, the manner of Terry in respect to the pistol provided for his service, and his quiet unconcern as to it and its shooting qualities, was evidence that he was acquainted with both of them.

The facts and circumstances already detailed, together with others to follow, establish to a moral certainty Terry's familiar knowledge of the weapons selected for the purpose of the duel, and also Broderick's entire ignorance respecting them, until the one provided for him was placed in his hands.

It is susceptible of proof that, only a short time before the Terry-Broderick duel was fought, Terry and Dr. Aylette repaired to the place of a farmer in San Joaquin County, where they practised shooting at a mark with the pistols in question.

Charles C. Knox, for many years a business man in Sacramento, states that Terry had in his possession the same pistols while a Justice of the Supreme Court, at the state capitol, and he further says that a few days before the Terry-Broderick duel, he was at Haywards, in Alameda County, and while there the stage coach arrived on its way from Stockton to Oakland, with Terry, Dr. Ash, and Dr. Aylette as passengers. At Haywards they were met by a large number of their friends, who had come in several carriages from Oakland, to whom Terry and his travelling companions exhibited the Aylette pistols, and then they were given in charge of some one or more of their Oakland friends. Mr. Knox says Mr. Hayward, the landlord of the place bearing his name, asked him : " What is up that brings together such a lot of Chivs ? "

Dr. Washington M. Ryer, a practising physician at Stockton in early times, says Terry was in the habit of practising with the Aylette pistols at his place in Stockton, in 1857.

Terry's friend, Mr. O'Meara, states that Terry, " in preparing for the affair, procured at Stockton the duelling pistols owned by Jo Beard, ex-Clerk of the Supreme Court, then in the possession of Dr. Dan Aylette," with which he made "two shots, hitting each time below the target. He tried them no more." Here Mr. O'Meara admits that Terry practised with the pistols, but limits his practice to two shots—no more. How he became so exactly informed he does not explain. He speaks with the positive directness of one who knows, as the *Fidus Achates* of Judge Terry in all his wanderings—his watchful attendant in all his secluded retreats.

Opposed to this array of facts and circumstances is the statement of Mr. Brooks, in his account of the Terry-Broderick duel, in which he says : " The pistols selected were of the duelling pattern and belonged to Dr. Aylette. Terry was no better acquainted with them than was Broderick." How Mr. Brooks is able to state so positively that Terry was no better acquainted with them than was Broderick, it is not easy to understand. He states what it is impossible for him to know. It is certain that the testimony of witnesses to facts which they know, is of more value than the statement of one who merely denies, without knowledge of the matter of which he speaks.

The evidence already produced more than tends to show that Terry was well acquainted with the Aylette pistols, by frequent use of them before they were brought into requisition on the field of the conflict. Upon this point it may be said the evidence is substantially conclusive.

From what the gunsmith testified before the Coroner's jury, there is no doubt respecting the dangerous character of the weapons, and especially of the one appointed to the lot of Broderick.

This account of the gunsmith was confirmed by what Mr. Broderick said on his dying bed, as appears further on.

Mr. O'Meara says the pistols in question had been used, before the Terry-Broderick duel, in " several affairs of honor ; " that they " were so exactly alike in every respect, that no difference had ever been discovered in their shooting qualities. They had hair-triggers, evenly and equally adjusted." The phrase " their shooting qualities ". is ambiguous. That their hair-triggers were evenly and equally adjusted is not sustained by the established facts. It is quite certain they were not evenly and equally adjusted on the morning when used by the two principals.

The next day after the duel transpired, the pistol which fell to the lot of Broderick came into the possession of the Captain of the Detective force of the police department of San Francisco, who experimented with it for the purpose of testing its alleged trigger infirmity. By a simple experiment, he demonstrated its extremely dangerous character in the hands of any one unaware of its eccentricity. With the hammer of the lock set, he caused it to spring by blowing vigorously from his mouth against the trigger. The success of the experiment was known at the time, and can now be proved by the Captain himself, who is still in the possession and enjoyment of a strong and retentive memory.

The peculiar and dangerous qualities of the respective weapons had been known for several years before, by those acquainted with them.

A few years before his death, Jo Beard, who at one time owned these pistols, told his friend Frederick H. Waterman, now residing in San Francisco, that there was something peculiar about these pistols—that they were not alike —that one of them was tricky, but the other was a lucky pistol that always killed. Jo Beard was a personal friend of Terry, in full sympathy with his pro-slavery views.

The same pistols were used in the duel between Dr. Washington M. Ryer and Dr. George Langdon, which occurred at Stockton, in 1857. Dr. Langdon, the challenged party, chose the Aylette pistols for the conflict. Each took one of them for the purpose of preparing in advance for the duel. Dr. Langdon selected for his use the weapon of stronger trigger. Dr. Ryer was then ignorant of the difference between them. In practising with the one that came to his hands he discovered its tricky character, but, with all his care in guarding against its eccentric characteristics, he was unable to fully overcome it. Afterwards, on the field, he said that, with all his caution, he was not able to bring his pistol to a horizontal position before it became discharged. At the third round he succeeded in raising it as high as the knee of his adversary, in which his third shot took effect and so ended that duel. Dr Ryer says that during the exchange of shots, the bullets from the pistol of Dr. Langdon whizzed unpleasantly past his ear, thus showing that the latter's pistol was not afflicted with the infirmity peculiar to his own.

Dr. Langdon was one of what was known at that day as the "Stockton Gang," at the head of which stood Terry as its acknowledged leader.

It is a significant fact that, in the cases in which the Aylette pistols were called into requisition, the one of stronger trigger was always found in the hands of the Terry school of duellists. Terry secured it in the duel which proved so fatal to Broderick, and Dr. Langdon secured it in the duel with Dr. Ryer.

Elliot J. Moore, for the last forty years a resident of San Francisco, a lawyer of highly reputable standing, and in early times a State Senator of admittted intelligence and integrity, was an intimate friend of Broderick, and was with him when the duel took place. He remembers the incidents of that bloody affair with a vividness which the lapse of time can never efface. He says that when the seconds of the respective principals, and others with them, were huddled together selecting pistols, he and Broderick were together some distance away. When Broderick became apprised of the fact that Terry's seconds had brought to the ground a pair of duelling pistols, and that the seconds of the two principals were then engaged in casting lots for the choice of weapons, he seemed uneasy and expressed himself as not being able to understand how it was that the armorer, selected by mutual consent of the parties, and then standing apart, was not consulted but seemed to be entirely ignored. Broderick had supposed the armorer was to provide the weapons for the occasion. He complained of the inefficiency of his seconds, who, he had become convinced, were not the equals of the seconds of his adversary. He spoke of them as children, and expressed apprehensions lest they might unwittingly "trade away his life."

It is evident that Broderick was not aware of Terry's acquaintance by practice with the pistols prior to the duel. The outspoken suspicions on the subject were withheld from him when on his dying bed. His experience with the weapon placed in his hands was to him a surprise and disappointment; for, while conscious that he could not recover, he told his friend Moore that he did not touch the trigger of the pistol as he raised it, but that the sudden movement in raising it caused it to explode before it was brought to a level.

Jo Beard's confession, the gunsmith's testimony, Dr. Ryer's statement, Broderick's dying declaration, and the Detective Captain's experiment, well establish the anomalous trigger qualities of the weapons, especially as to the one assigned to Broderick. In addition to this direct proof are the circumstances of the production and selection by Terry and his friends of their favorite and cherished weapons, and their extreme care to secure the safer one for his use.

Terry's friend, Mr. O'Meara, states the fact to be that the respective parties mutually agreed upon the employment of the gunsmith as armorer for the Terry-Broderick duel. Of this fact there seems no reason for doubt. But on the ground, the armorer was required to stand aside, except that he was allowed to examine the pistols chosen, and to load the one handed over by Terry's seconds for Broderick's use.

Col. William W. Gift was a Democrat, reared in Tennessee under the immediate influence of General Andrew Jackson. He was widely known in California for his peculiar and forcible modes of expressing his opinions. Immediately after Broderick was shot down, he gave vent to his indignation, and denounced in strong language the management of the Terry party in their introduction and selection of the pistols in question for the purposes of the duel. He declared that Terry had told him that he himself owned the pistols. Col. Gift was a believer in the Code, but regarded it as a system which required fair and equal dealing between parties engaged in "affairs of honor."

The facts and circumstances of the choosing of the Aylette pistols, and the selecting of the safer one for Terry and the dangerous one for Broderick, as the same became known, caused it to be suspected and believed by the people that Broderick had fallen the victim of a foul conspiracy—that a tricky pistol had been placed in his grasp, untutored to its eccentricity, in order to make sure of his discomfiture in an unequal wager of battle.

Indicative of the general suspicions, the following inquiries were publicly made, which are quoted as showing the general belief that then prevailed.

"Why was the duel fought with Judge Terry's pistols?"

"Did Broderick or his seconds know they were the property of Judge Terry?"

"Was either of the pistols so arranged as to go off with the lesser jar or shake without touching the trigger? If so, was either Mr. Broderick or his seconds aware of it?"

"By whom were the pistols selected, or were they furnished by the armorer as his property?"

"Did not Judge Terry practise with these pistols within forty-eight hours of the time of Mr. Broderick's being shot?"

These inquiries were made in the "Alta," followed by a suggestion in the nature of a request, in these words: "Direct answers to these questions by the proper parties will prove what are now said to be the facts, false or true." At this time Mr. Broderick was no more.

Terry and his friends did not deign to answer these questions. McKibben and Colton had already said, in noticing an article in the San Francisco "Herald" to the effect that one of the weapons was easier on the trigger than the other: "Had we believed there was any unfairness, there could have been no meeting." But the armorer testified at the Coroner's inquest that the pistols were extremely light and delicate on the trigger, and that he so informed *all the seconds* when he examined them on the ground, and that he told one of Terry's seconds that the one designed for Broderick was lighter than the other.

The belief which so greatly obtained immediately after Broderick was shot, that he had fallen the victim of foul play, has remained with those best informed on the subject even to the present time, and on all occasions when the opportunity occurred to give expression to such belief, it has been manifested in a pronounced manner An instance of the kind occurred at the presidential election in 1880, when Terry was a Democratic candidate for presidential elector. At the election in November of that year, all the Democratic candidates were chosen except Terry, who fell behind and was defeated, by a respectable majority, by Henry Edgerton, one of the Republican nominees for elector, who, in the state electoral college, cast his vote for Garfield and Arthur. Edgerton was an anti-Lecompton Democrat in 1859, and was well known among the friends of Broderick to have been in sympathy with him. The friends of Broderick remaining in the Democratic party, remembering him as their leader and how he came to his untimely end, would not tolerate Terry as worthy to express, as an elector, their choice for the offices of President and Vice-President of the United States.

It appears beyond question that Terry possessed a great and undue advantage over Broderick in respect to the weapons used. He had had long and familiar acquaintance with them, while, as to their peculiar qualities, Broderick was an entire stranger.

It has been claimed by some that Broderick was more expert in the use of duelling pistols than was Terry. If this be true, the result of the hostile meeting, so fatal to

Broderick, must be accounted for on the hypothesis of some undue advantage on the side of Terry.

The claim that Broderick was more skilful and expert in the use of duelling pistols than was Terry, cannot be affirmed by those acquainted with the two men. Terry was known to be familiar with, and ready in the use of, such weapons. Besides this, the training of his life had made him familiar with duelling weapons. The advantages of an experience in the use of arms were clearly on his side.

The environments of the early lives of the respective parties were entirely different. The one had spent his youth and early manhood in New York, where the use of pistols in duelling conflicts was unknown. The other had spent his early life in Texas, famous for scenes of violence and blood. His early opportunities gave him a general experience in affairs of violence which had not been afforded to Broderick.

To this comparative difference Col. Baker, in his eloquent oration at Broderick's funeral, made allusion. He said: "The Code of Honor is a delusion and a snare. It palters with the hope of a true courage, and binds it at the feet of crafty and cruel skill. It surrounds its victim with the pomp and grace of a procession, but leaves him bleeding on the altar. It substitutes cold and deliberate preparation for courageous and manly impulse, and arms the one to disarm the other. It may prevent fraud among practised duellists, who should be forever without its pale, but it makes the mere 'trick of the weapon' superior to the noblest cause and truest courage. Its pretence of equality is a lie; it is equal in all the form, it is unequal in all the substance. The habitude of arms—the early training—the frontier life—the border war—the sectional custom—the life of leisure,—all these are advantages which no negotiations can neutralize, and which no courage can overcome."

Here it is to be noticed that the orator's mind was impressed with the prevailing suspicions and beliefs, as he spoke of "cruel and crafty skill"—of the "substitution of cold and deliberate preparation for courageous and manly impulse"—and the "' mere trick of the weapon' superior to the noblest cause and truest courage."

The usual answer given to the suggestion that Broderick was overreached and defrauded in respect to the weapons selected for the duel has been, that his seconds must be presumed to have guarded against any undue advantage in favor of his adversary. This, at most, is only a presumption which is disputable. The facts and circumstances seem to overthrow any such presumption. They ought to have guarded against any such advantage. But their failure to do so cannot be tolerated as a justification or excuse for bringing on the ground weapons of the dangerous character of the Aylette pistols, with which Terry was familiar, and Broderick wholly ignorant. The selection of those pistols was taking an undue advantage of Broderick, which was intensified by the selection of the stronger one for Terry and the weaker one for Broderick.

Mr. Broderick was entitled to fair dealing. His seconds ought to have been on the alert, and guarded their principal against the very things which happened so greatly to the advantage of Terry, and to the disadvantage of Broderick, but they failed to do so. Were they overmatched and outdone by the seconds of Terry? It is quite manifest they were. They were inexperienced in matters of the kind, and evidently supposed the affair in hand an "affair of honor." They ought to have been on the alert and attended to what the gunsmith told them as to the dangerous character of the weapons, and thus been able to defeat the strategic circumventions of their principal's adversaries. This opportunity was lost, and as a consequence all was lost. They probably were without suspicion of Terry's advantage, until it was too late to repair the loss to their principal.

It has been stated in several of the published accounts of the Terry-Broderick duel, that McKibben snapped one of the Aylette pistols with an air of satisfaction ; but this is not supported by the testimony of the living witnesses. If he did, then which of the pistols did he snap with a satisfied air? If he did snap one of them, is it proof that the pistol delivered to Broderick for use was not extremely light, and dangerously set? The armorer said it was, and so light that it would explode by a sudden jar or jerk ; and Mr. Broderick declared on his dying bed that, without his touching the trigger, it did explode as he suddenly raised it.

In Maj. Ben. C. Truman's account of the duel, it is said, in speaking of the managing friends of the respective principals, "As to the niceties of affairs of honor, the gentlemen who assisted Terry were much superior to Broderick's friends ;" and in speaking of their bearing and conduct on the field, it is further said, "The Terry party was cool and collected, as became old hands at the business. Mr. Broderick's friends were apparently nervous and hesitating." Their nervous and disturbed condition may account for their consenting to the negotiations by which the Aylette pistols were allowed to be introduced for choice, and for their failure, after such pistols were chosen by Terry, to attend to the warning of the gunsmith that they were too light for the purposes of the duel, and also for their failure to discover that the one selected by Terry's seconds for him was the stronger and safer of the two, and that the one handed over for Broderick's use was so light and delicate as to be discharged by a sudden jar or jerk.

The evidence as to the dangerous character of the weapons and the more dangerous character of the one used by Broderick, is the sworn testimony of the gunsmith, Legardo, at the Coroner's inquest, which has never been contradicted.

The evidence relating to the point under consideration is both direct and circumstantial, and from it the conclusion follows in logical sequence.

The great and fatal mistake of Broderick's seconds, was in submitting to a negotiation which opened the door to the selection of any pistols not provided by the armorer, upon whom the respective parties had mutually agreed for the purpose. The arrangement to that effect operated to set aside the agreement mutually entered into to employ the gunsmith, Legardo, for the office of armorer. The death of Mr. Broderick, it is believed by many, was the consequence of this fatal mistake.

By persistent asseverations, made in the face of the evidence to the contrary, the duel has been represented as fair and equal in all respects, and Broderick's seconds have contributed their full share to so represent it. Perhaps they thought so; but Broderick's friends have ever, with great unanimity, thought otherwise.

The personal treatment of Broderick from the beginning to the end by his antagonist and his second, Benham, in arousing him from his sleep at the house of his friend at the dead hour of the night, and the mode and manner of the examination of his person on the field of the conflict, seemed designed to worry and wear him out, and to unnerve and unfit him for the ordeal in prospect. Added to such treatment, the introduction on the ground of the Aylette pistols, and their selection and distribution for the work in hand, made sure of Broderick's discomfiture and death.

All the facts and circumstances considered, the following questions are propounded:

Was there any just or sufficient cause, under the Code, for the challenge by Terry to Broderick?

Which of the two was the first to give offence to the other, and which was bound in honor to make apology and reparation to the other?

Were the Aylette pistols proper duelling weapons for the purposes of the Terry-Broderick duel?

Were they unsafe and dangerous weapons in the hands of a stranger to their peculiar characteristics?

Was Terry familiar with them, by actual experience, within a short time before the duel?

Was Broderick acquainted with them, or was he entirely ignorant respecting their peculiar qualities?

Did Terry secure for his use the safer pistol of the two, knowing the character of both?

Was the pistol given to Broderick for his use a particularly dangerous weapon, and were Terry and his aiding friends aware of such fact?

Were Terry's friends aware of the facts and circumstances relating to the character of the pistols, and of the difference between them?

Were the facts in respect to Terry's acquaintance with and experimental knowledge of the pistols, concealed by him and his friends from Broderick and his friends?

Truthful answers to these questions will constitute a true verdict according to the evidence, on which judgment must be pronounced, declaring who was responsible for the untimely death of David C. Broderick—who answerable for the deep damnation of his taking off.

SAN FRANCISCO, ———, 1890.

ORATION

OF

COLONEL EDWARD D. BAKER

OVER THE DEAD BODY OF

DAVID C. BRODERICK,

A SENATOR OF THE UNITED STATES,

DELIVERED ON SEPTEMBER 18TH, 1859.

David C. Broderick was shot in a duel on the thirteenth of September, 1859, and died three days thereafter, on the sixteenth. The challenging party was David S. Terry, who, five days prior to the meeting, resigned his office as Chief-Justice of California—having then but a few weeks to serve. The funeral service was held in the plaza of San Francisco, on Sunday the eighteenth, when Colonel Baker, standing by the open coffin, delivered the following address. It was heard by a very large concourse of people and produced a great effect. It is now reprinted in the hope of preserving a worthy memorial of two eminent persons—Senator Broderick and Colonel Edward D. Baker, some time Senator from Oregon, and an early victim of the causeless Rebellion.

CITIZENS OF CALIFORNIA: A Senator lies dead in our midst. He is wrapped in a bloody shroud, and we, to whom his toils and cares were given, are about to bear him to the place appointed for all the living. It is not fit that such a man should pass to the tomb unheralded; it is not fit that such a life should steal away unnoticed to its close; it is not fit that such a death should call forth no rebuke, or be surrounded by no public lamentation. It is this conviction which impels the gathering of this assemblage. We are here of every station and pursuit, of every creed and character, each in his capacity of citizen, to swell the mournful tribute which the majesty of the people offers to the unreplying dead. He lies to-day surrounded by little of funeral pomp. No banners droop above the bier; no melancholy music floats upon the reluctant air. The hopes of highhearted friends droop like the fading flowers upon his breast, and the struggling sigh compels the tear in eyes that seldom weep. Around him are those who have known him best and loved him longest; who have shared the triumph and endured the defeat. Near him are the gravest and noblest of the State, possessed by a grief at once earnest and sincere; while beyond, the masses of the people, whom he loved and for whom his life was given, gather like a thunder-cloud of swelling and indignant grief. In such a presence, fellow-citizens, let us linger for a moment at the portals of the tomb, whose shadowy arches vibrate to the public heart, to speak a few brief words of the man, of his life, and of his death.

Mr. Broderick was born in the District of Columbia in 1819; he was of Irish descent and of respectable though obscure parentage; he had little of early advantages, and never summoned to his aid a complete and finished education. His boyhood—as, indeed, his early manhood—was passed in the City of New York, and the loss of his father early stimulated him to the efforts which maintained his surviving mother and brother, and served also to fix and form his character even in his boyhood. His love for his mother was his first and most distinctive trait of character; and when his brother died—an early and sudden death—the shock gave a serious and reflective cast to his habits and his thoughts, which marked them to the last hour of his life.

He was always filled with pride and energy and ambition; his pride was in the manliness and force of his character, and no man had more reason. His energy was manifest in the most resolute struggles with poverty and obscurity, and his ambition impelled him to seek a foremost place in the great race for honorable power. Up to the time of his arrival in California, his life had been passed amid events incident to such a character. Fearless, self-reliant, open in his enmities, warm in his friendships, wedded to his opinion, and marching directly to his purpose through and over all opposition, his career was chequered with success and defeat. But even in defeat his energies were strengthened and his character developed. When he reached these shores his keen observation taught him at once that he trod a broad field, and that a higher career was before him. He had no false pride—sprung from a people and of a race whose vocation was labor, he toiled with his own hands and sprang at a bound from the workshop to the legislative hall. From that hour there congregated around him and against him the elements of success and defeat. Strong friendships, bitter enmities, high praise, malignant calumnies; but he trod with a free and a proud step that onward path which has led him to glory and the grave.

It would be idle for me at this hour, and in this place, to speak of all that history with unmitigated praise; it will be idle for his enemies hereafter to deny his claim to noble virtues and high purposes. When, in the Legislature, he

boldly denounced the special legislation which is the curse
of a new country, he proved his courage and his rectitude.
When he opposed the various and sometimes successful
schemes to strike out the salutary provisions of the constitution which guarded free labor, he was true to all the better
instincts of his life. When, prompted by his ambition and
the admiration of his friends, he first sought a seat in the
Senate of the United States, he sought the highest of all
positions by legitimate effort, and failed with honor. It is
my duty to say that, in my judgment, when, at a later period,
he sought to anticipate the Senatorial election, he committed
an error, which, I think, he lived to regret. It would have
been a violation of the true principles of representative government, which no reason, public or private, could justify,
and could never have met the permanent approval of good
and wise men. Yet, while I say this over his bier, let me
remind you of the temptation to such an error, of the plans
and the reasons which prompted it, of the many good purposes it was intended to effect. And if ambition, "the last
infirmity of noble minds," led him for a moment from the
better path, let me remind you how nobly he retained it.

It is impossible to speak, within the limits of this address,
of the events of that session of the Legislature at which he
was elected to the Senate of the United States ; but some
things should not be passed in silence here. The contest
between himself and the present Senator had been bitter
and personal. He had triumphed ; he had been wonderfully
sustained by his friends, and stood confessedly "the first in
honor and the first in place." He yielded to an appeal made
to his magnanimity by his foe. If he judged unwisely, he
has paid the forfeit well. Never in the history of political
warfare has any man been so pursued. Never has malignity
so exhausted itself. Fellow-citizens, the man who lies before
you was your Senator. From the moment of his election,
his character has been maligned, his motives attacked, his
courage impeached, his patriotism assailed. It has been a

system tending to one end, *and the end is here.* What was his crime? Review his history—consider his public acts— weigh his private character—and before the grave encloses him forever, judge between him and his enemies. As a man to be judged in his private relations, who was his superior? It was his boast—and amid the general license of a new country it was a proud one—that his most scrutinizing enemy could fix no single act of immorality upon him. Temperate, decorous, self-restrained, he had passed through all the excitements of California unstained. No man could charge him with broken faith or violated trust. Of habits simple and inexpensive, he had no lust of gain. He overreached no man's weakness in a bargain, and withheld no man his just due. Never, in the history of the State, has there been a citizen who has borne public relations more stainless in all respects than he. But it is not by this standard he is to be judged. He was a public man, and his memory demands a public judgment. What was his public crime? The answer is in his own words: "They have killed me because I was opposed to the extension of slavery and a corrupt Administration." Fellow-citizens, they are remarkable words, uttered at a very remarkable moment; they involve the history of his Senatorial career, and of its sad and bloody termination. When Mr. Broderick entered the Senate he had been elected at the beginning of a Presidential term, as a friend of the President-elect, having undoubtedly been one of his most influential supporters. There were unquestionably some things in the exercise of the appointing power which he could have wished otherwise; but he had every reason with the Administration which could be supposed to weigh with a man in his position. He had heartily maintained the doctrine of popular sovereignty as set forth in the Cincinnati platform, and he never wavered in its support till the day of his death. But when in his judgment the President betrayed his obligations to the party and the country—when, in the whole series of acts in relation to

Kansas, he proved recreant to his pledges and instructions; when the whole power of the Administration was brought to bear upon the legislative branch of the Government in order to force slavery upon an unwilling people, then in the high performance of his duty as a Senator, he rebuked the Administration by his voice and his vote, and stood by his principles. It is true he adopted no half-way measures. He threw the whole weight of his character into the ranks of the opposition; he endeavored to rouse the people to an indignant sense of the iniquitous tyranny of the Federal power, and kindling with the contest, became its fiercest and firmest opponent.

Fellow-citizens, whatever may have been your political predilections, it is impossible to repress your admiration as you review the conduct of the man who lies hushed in death before you. You read in his history a glorious imitation of the great popular leaders who opposed the despotic influence of power in other lands and in our own. When John Hampden died at Chalgrove Field he sealed his devotion to popular liberty with his blood. The eloquence of Fox found the sources of its inspiration in his love of the people. When Senators conspired against Tiberius Gracchus and the Tribune of the people fell beneath their daggers, it was power that prompted the crime and demanded the sacrifice. Who can doubt if your Senator had surrendered his free thoughts and bent in submission to the rule of the Administration—who can doubt that instead of resting on a bloody bier, he would this day have been reposing in the inglorious felicitude of Presidential sunshine?

Fellow-citizens, let no man suppose that the death of the eminent citizen of whom I speak was caused by any other reason than that to which his own words assign it. It had been long foreshadowed. It was predicted by his friends; it was threatened by his enemies; it was the consequence of intense political hatred. His death was a political necessity, poorly veiled under the guise of a private quarrel. Here, in his own State, among those who witnessed the late canvass, who knew the contending leaders—among those who knew the antagonists on the bloody ground, here the public conviction is so thoroughly settled that nothing need be said. Tested by the correspondence itself, there was no cause in morals, in honor, in taste, by any code—by the custom of any civilized land, there was no cause for blood. Let me repeat the story; it is as brief as it is fatal: A judge of the Supreme Court descends into a political convention—it is just, however, to say that the occasion was to return thanks to his friends for an unsuccessful support; in a speech bitter and personal he stigmatized Senator Broderick and all his friends in words of contemptuous insult. When Mr. Broderick saw that speech he retorted, saying, in substance, that he had heretofore spoken of Judge Terry as an honest man, but that he now took it back. When inquired of, he admitted that he had so said, and connected his words with Judge Terry's speech as prompting them. So far as Judge Terry personally was concerned, this was the cause of mortal combat; there was no other. In the contest which has just terminated in the State, Mr. Broderick had taken a leading part; he had been engaged in controversies very personal in their nature, because the subjects of public discussion had involved the character and conduct of many public and distinguished men. But Judge Terry was not one of these. He was no contestant; his conduct was not in issue; he had been mentioned but once incidentally—in reply to his own attack—and, except as it might be found in his peculiar traits or peculiar fitness, there was no reason to suppose that he would seek any man's blood. When William of Nassau, the deliverer of Holland, died in the presence of his wife and children, the hand that struck the blow was not nerved by private vengeance. When the fourth Henry passed unharmed amid the dangers of the field of Ivry, to perish in the streets of his capital by the hand of a fanatic, he did not seek to avenge a private grief. An exaggerated sense of personal honor—a weak mind with choleric passions, intense sectional prejudice, united with great confidence in the use of arms—these sometimes serve to stimulate the instruments which accomplish the deepest and deadliest purpose.

Fellow-citizens! one year ago I performed a duty such as I perform to-day over the remains of Senator Ferguson, who died as Broderick died, tangled in the meshes of the code of honor. To-day there is another and more eminent sacrifice. To-day I renew my protest; to-day I utter yours. The code of honor is a delusion and a snare; it palters with the hope of a true courage, and binds it at the feet of crafty and cruel skill. It surrounds its victim with the pomp and grace of the procession, but leaves him bleeding on the altar. It substitutes cold and deliberate preparation for courageous and manly impulse, and arms the one to disarm the other; it may prevent fraud between practised duellists who should be forever without its pale, but it makes the mere "trick of the weapon" superior to the noblest cause and the truest courage. Its pretence of equality is a lie; it is equal in all the form, it is unequal in all the substance—the habitude of arms, the early training, the frontier life, the border war, the sectional custom, the life of leisure—all these are advantages which no negotiations can neutralize, and which no courage can overcome. But, fellow-citizens, the protest is not only spoken in your words and mine—it is written in indelible characters; it is written in the blood of Gilbert, in the blood of Ferguson, in the blood of Broderick, and the inscription will not altogether fade. With the administration of the code in this particular case I am not here to deal. Amid passionate grief let us strive to be just. I give no currency to rumors of which personally I know nothing; there are other tribunals to which they may well be referred, and this is not one of them; but I am here to say that whatever in the code of honor or out of it demands or allows a deadly combat, where there is not in all things entire and certain equality, is a prostitution of the name, is an evasion of the substance, and is a shield blazoned with the name of chivalry to cover the malignity of murder.

And now the shadows turn toward the East, and we prepare to bear these poor remains to their silent resting-place. Let us not seek to repress the generous pride which prompts a recital of noble deeds and manly virtues. He rose unaided and alone; he began his career without family or fortune, in the face of difficulties; he inherited poverty and obscurity; he died a Senator in Congress, having written his name in the history of the great struggle for the rights of the people against the despotism of organization and the corruption of power. He leaves in the hearts of his friends the tenderest and the proudest recollections. He was honest, faithful, earnest, sincere, generous, and brave; he felt in all the great crises of his life that he was a leader in the ranks, and for the rights of the masses of men, and he could not falter. When he returned from that fatal field, while the dark wing of the archangel of death was casting its shadows upon his brow, his greatest anxiety was as to the performance of his duty. He felt that all his strength and all his life belonged to the cause to which he had devoted them. "Baker," said he—and to me they were his last words—"Baker, when I was struck, I tried to stand firm, but the blow blinded me, and I could not." I trust that it is no shame to my manhood that tears blinded me as he said it. Of his last hours I have no heart to speak. He was the last of his race; there was no kindred hand to smooth his couch, or wipe the death-damps from his brow; but around that dying bed strong men, the friends of early manhood, the devoted adherents of later life, bowed in irrepressible grief, and lifted up their voices and wept.

But, fellow-citizens, the voice of lamentation is not uttered by private friendship alone—the blow that struck his manly breast has touched the heart of a people, and as the sad tidings spread a general gloom prevails. Who now can speak for California? Who can be the interpreter of the wants of the Pacific coast? Who can appeal to the communities of the Atlantic, who love free labor? Who can speak for the masses of men, with a passionate love for the classes from whence he sprung? Who can defy the blandishments of power, the indolence of office, the corruption of administrations? What hopes are buried with him in the grave?

"Ah! who that gallant spirit shall resume,
Leap from Eurotas' bank and call us from the tomb?"

But the last word must be spoken, and the imperious mandate of death must be fulfilled. Thus, O brave heart, we bear thee to thy rest! Thus, surrounded by tens of thousands, we leave thee to the equal grave. As in life no other voice among us so rang its trumpet-blast upon the ear of freemen, so in death its echoes will reverberate amid our mountains and valleys, until truth and valor cease to appeal to the human heart.

"His love of truth—too warm, too strong,
For hope or fear to chain or chill,
His hate of tyranny and wrong
Burn in the breasts he kindled still."

Good friend! true hero! hail and farewell.

www.ingramcontent.com/pod-product-compliance
Lightning Source LLC
Chambersburg PA
CBHW032140270626
47172CB00009B/781